Published by
Kakao förlag
Stadt Hamburgsgatan 9B
211 38 Malmö
Sweden
www.kakao.se

Text: Anita Shenoi
Printing: DZS Grafik, Slovenia
via Italgraf Media, 2013
ISBN 9789185861705

AN A-Z AND BEYOND

Sweden

ANITA SHENOI • KAKAO FÖRLAG

CAN A NATION BE SUMMED UP BY THE LETTERS OF ITS ALPHABET?

Sweden: an A-Z and Beyond rises to the challenge by taking you on a whirlwind tour of key concepts that characterise the country and its people.

Especially designed for the inquisitive reader in a hurry, each letter and chapter is a launch pad of interesting facts, language tips and beautiful photographs to motivate further exploration of all things Swedish. And since there are three extra letters in the Swedish alphabet, you'll find this A-Z goes beyond the expected!

I've spent a long time enjoying the sights, sounds and feel of Sweden – I hope this book inspires you to do the same!

Anita Shenoi

ALLEMANSRÄTT [al:emansræt:]
RIGHT OF PUBLIC ACCESS

Setting up camp by a lake as the sun goes down, filling a basket with mushrooms and berries while you stroll through the woods – these are activities that many Swedes take for granted as they exercise *allemansrätt*, the unwritten law preserving freedom of movement ever since Viking times.

Freedom does not come without responsibility, however, and the recent rise of commercial berry picking in Sweden has led to fears this right is being abused, and is the subject of common debate. What does *allemansrätt* entail then, and are there restrictions?

GENERAL RIGHTS
• You may move through the woods and open landscape and use the lakes and rivers for swimming or boating.
• You may pick wild berries, mushrooms and some kinds of flowers, unless a certain species is protected by law.
• You may camp anywhere for one night (apart from the beach) so long as you do not disturb the local residents.

DON'T DISTURB, DON'T DESTROY
This is your responsibility in exercising allemansrätt, and involves thinking about things like:

Keeping control of your dog while out and about Between March 1st and August 20th dogs are not allowed to run loose as it is a sensitive period for wildlife.

Leaving your car behind There is no right of public access for motorised vehicles and it is forbidden to drive cars, motorcycles, mopeds on bare ground in the terrain.

Taking your rubbish with you If you have a barbecue or camp for the night, leave the area as undisturbed as you found it. Choose a safe place to light your fire, and make sure it is thoroughly extinguished before you leave.

Asking permission You may have the right to roam but respect private landowners by asking their permission when appropriate, especially if you wish to camp on their land. Don't camp too close to private residences and do not cross or occupy someone's yard.

Kebenekaise, meaning cauldron crest in the indigenous Sámi language of Lapland, is the highest mountain in Sweden

Sarek – for the wild at heart

For the most intrepid of explorers, a real challenge presents itself in Sarek – 197,000 hectares of national park, fifty kilometres east of the Norwegian border in the northern county of Norrbotten. Comprising dramatic mountain ranges and narrow valleys, glaciers and wild rapids, Sarek is a breathtaking area of unspoiled wilderness. Six of Sweden's 13 highest mountains are found here, as well as about 100 glaciers. It is not for the beginner, however. There are no tourist facilities in the park whatsoever, and the alpine terrain and rapidly changing weather can cause hikers severe difficulties without the right experience and equipment. But if you've ever dreamt of facing the raw elements and testing your survival skills in a true wilderness, this is the place to go.

BLÅBÄR [blo:bæ:r]

BILBERRIES

Sweet, tart and dripping with deep blue pigment, bilberries are perhaps the most beloved of edible treasures be found in Swedish forests. Distinct from its North American cousin, the blueberry, Vaccinium myrtillus L. is smaller, more delicate and notoriously difficult to cultivate, meaning it remains a truly wild treat.

Purple lips and inky fingers are the prize for many Swedes returning from a foraging expedition to their local woods – and if they're lucky they will have saved a few berries for their baskets too. These will have to be eaten as soon as possible, or preserved as jam or syrup to be savoured during the colder winter months.

But the popularity of the Swedish bilberry does not rest with natives alone. With wild bilberries much sought after by the health-food industry, thousands of workers from Asia and elsewhere arrive in Sweden during the summer months to work for commercial berry companies – an influx that is causing controversy over cheap labour and poor working conditions. The workers themselves are none too happy either; when berries are scarce, many cannot cover the cost of their stay, causing huge problems for local communities. As Sweden grapples with this new phenomenon, its famously worker-friendly regulations are being tested to the max!

Berry-licious
Did you know Swedes make bilberries into a soup? *Blåbärssoppa* is a comforting hot drink and a favourite for the Thermos on winter sports outings!

Berry-good
Rich in flavonoids and anthocyanins, the bilberry is an antioxidant powerhouse. Consumed fresh, preserved or as an extract, the fruit is widely reputed to support eye function, enhance vascular health and help in managing diabetes.

B

Speak the lingo: Double Trouble

Ett riktigt blåbär!

In Swedish, if someone calls you a 'blueberry', they mean you're an absolute beginner!

The term was originally coined in the 1960s to describe less-talented participants of the famous Vasaloppet ski-race who crossed the finishing line covered in blue stains – they'd had one too many stop-offs for bilberry soup!

BILBERRIES AREN'T THE ONLY FRUIT...

Swedish forests are a larder full of delectable delicacies for the keen forager. In addition to bilberries you may find:

LINGON
Lingonberry, similar to the cranberry, is another super fruit laden with antioxidants, its antibacterial properties also being said to help fight infections of the urinary tract. Lingonberry jam is a staple condiment for many Swedish dishes.

HJORTRON
The beautiful yellow cloudberry is an elusive prize, thriving on inaccessible marshland, particularly in the north of Sweden. Heaven on a plate with waffles or ice-cream, cloudberry jam is one of the best ways to enjoy the fruit. 'Forest gold' won't come cheap though – fresh berries can fetch upwards of SEK100 per kilo.

KANTARELLER
Mounds of golden chanterelles, sometimes known as girolles, are a feast for the eyes at many an outdoor market in Sweden during the summer. Simply pan-fried in butter or with a splash of cream, the mushrooms are revered for their delicate yet complex flavour.

CELSIUS [selsius]
CELSIUS

Most famous for helping the world understand temperature in °C from 0-100, the Swedish scientist Anders Celsius (1701-1744) was also noted for his outstanding work as an astronomer. At a time in history when blind beliefs were beginning to be challenged, Celsius stood out as a masterful observer of the natural world, bringing important facts to light.

Among his many contributions to science, Celsius' work on the Aurora Borealis brought him international acclaim. He and his assistant, Olof Hiorter first realized that the phenomenon has magnetic causes, simply by observing the deviations of a compass needle during aurora activity.

BRIEF LIFE, LASTING IMPACT
Although Celsius died of tuberculosis at only 42, he managed in his short life time to help change the way we perceive the world. Among other things he:

• Participated in the famous 'Lapland Expedition' (1736), which aimed to measure the length of a degree along a meridian close to the pole and compare the result with a similar expedition close to the equator. The expeditions confirmed Newton's belief that the shape of the Earth was an ellipsoid, flattened at the poles.

• Proposed the temperature scale which takes his name, originally with 0° as the boiling point of water and 100° as the freezing point (1742). The scale was reversed in 1745 for more practical usage.

• Actively worked to introduce the Gregorian calendar in Sweden but wasn't successful until 1753, almost a decade after his death.

Anders Celsius

*Like a magic curtain sweeping the polar sky, the Aurora Borealis
has fascinated people since time began. See p.55 for more on this*

THREE MORE BRIGHT SPARKS
IN THE AGE OF ENLIGHTENMENT

CARL LINNAEUS (1707-1778)

This botanist extraordinaire laid the foundations for our modern system of plant and animal classification after his extensive work surveying flora and fauna in Sweden and abroad. His two most famous works, *Species Plantarum* (1753) and *Systema naturae* (10th edition, 1758), are internationally recognized as the starting points for botanical and zoological nomenclature respectively.

EMANUEL SWEDENBORG (1688-1772)

Science, theology and mysticism were all encompassed in the prolific works of the visionary Swedenborg, whose ideas went on to influence important figures such as Immanuel Kant, William Blake and Carl Jung. Swedenborg's diverse achievements ranged from designing mechanical inventions such as a submarine, making discoveries about the brain and nervous system way ahead of his time, and his most famous work, *Heaven and Hell* (1758), an account of his spiritual 'next world' experiences.

CARL WILHELM SCHEELE (1742-1786)

Of German-Swedish descent, Scheele started out as an apprentice pharmacist in Gothenburg, before practising as a fully fledged chemist in various locations around Sweden. At a time when lots of exciting chemical discoveries were being made, Scheele often missed out on recognition among his contemporaries because he published his findings too late. His discovery of oxygen, for example, was made a number of years before that of Joseph Priestly and Lavoisier, and Scheele is now also accredited with discovering other important elements such as barium and tungsten. Perhaps his most commercially ground-breaking discovery, however, was a method of mass-producing phosphorous, which led to Sweden becoming one of the world's leading producers of matches.

Karl von Linné.

Carl Linnaeus

One man's discovery lit up the world for many

The twin flower, Linnaea, which was named in honour of the great scientist. Linnea is a popular girls' name in Sweden

DECKARE [dæk:are]
CRIME FICTION

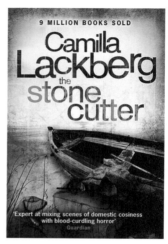

You know you've arrived as an author when the likes of Daniel Craig and Kenneth Branagh are called in to portray your protagonists on the silver screen. And it seems the spotlight is still shining on Sweden's crime writers, long after the smash hits of Stieg Larsson's Millennium trilogy and Henning Mankell's Wallander have reached the pinnacle of success.

But what's so great about Swedish whodunnits? Complex psychological scenarios, moody, isolated settings and less-than-perfect detectives with existential angst are some of the ingredients capturing the imagination of millions of readers worldwide. While few would accuse Sweden of being a hot-bed of real-life crime, a hot-house for fictitious villainy it certainly is.

Just one of Camilla Läckberg's top-selling titles

The quaint streets of Ystad, home to Wallander's not-so quaint crime investigations

NAMES YOU MAY KNOW

CAMILLA LÄCKBERG

Debuting with *The Ice Princess* in 2003, Camilla is most famous for her Fjällbacka series, set in the Swedish west-coast village where she was born and raised. The rights to Läckberg's books have been sold in over 30 countries. **Latest novel:** *Änglamakarskan* (*The Angel Maker*)

LIZA MARKLUND

Depicting the helter-skelter lifestyle of a tabloid report-er is Liza's speciality, her Annika Bengtzon novels having sold millions of copies worldwide. In 2010, *The Postcard Killers*, co-written with James Patterson saw Marklund reaching No.1 on the New York Times bestseller list. **Latest novel:** *Du Gamla, Du Fria* (*Borderline*)

HÅKAN NESSER

Long experience as a teacher of Swedish and English has made Håkan the devil for detail in his writing career. Best known for his Van Vetereen and Barbarotti series, Nesser won the European Crime Fic-tion Award, affectionately known as the 'Ripper Award,' in 2010. **Latest novel:** *Styckerskan från Lilla Burma* (*The Butcheress from Little Burma*)

Not forgetting...

SJÖWALL-WAHLÖÖ
The couple's Martin Beck series from 1965–1975 gave them a place in history as the found-ers of modern Scandinavian crime fiction

MARI JUNGSTEDT
The Dead of Summer was no.1 Crime Bestseller in the USA in July 2012

KARIN ALVTEGEN
Missing was nominated for the prestigious Edgar Award for Best Novel in 2009

D

SUPER SLEUTH CHALLENGE

The mystery: Tim Davys is the pseudonym for a Swedish author who wrote the *Mollison Town quartet*, four works of existentialist noir set in a town inhabited exclusively by stuffed animals. Can you reveal the true identity of the author?

NAMES TO WATCH

JENS LAPIDUS

The criminal defence lawyer turned crime writer has impressed with his Stockholm Noir trilogy starting with *Snabba Cash* (*Easy Money*). Already filmatized in Swedish by Daniel Espinosa (2010), a Hollywood remake is on the cards.

MONS KALLENTOFT

Turning his Mid-Sweden working-class upbringing around on its head, Kallentoft has revealed true literary talent. His novels about boundary-pushing Superintendent Malin Fors have been translated into 16 languages. *Midvinterblod* (*Midwinter Sacrifice*) was published in the UK in 2011.

JOHAN THEORIN

Just three books into his spooky quartet set in the wild and wonderful landscape of Öland, Theorin appears to be holding his own as an international crime writer, winning the CWA International Dagger prize in 2010 with his second book, *Nattfåk* (*The Darkest Room*).

Jens Lapidus makes crime writing look like easy money...

Johan Theorin, master of the dark and mysterious

ERIKSSON [erikson]
ERIKSSON

Svensson, Karlsson, Jansson, Eriksson... many Swedish surnames end in -son, the legacy of an ancient Scandinavian naming practice that was not abolished until 1901, with the Names Adoption Act. Until then, many Swedes had 'surnames' composed of their father's name, plus an affix denoting the relationship with him, for example Jan Eriksson (Jan, son of Erik) or Anna Eriksdotter (Anna, daughter of Erik). In this case, the Names Act implied scrapping Eriksdotter and adopting Eriksson as the family name, assuring there would be generations of Erikssons to come.

Nevertheless, evidence of the simple Viking approach to family relationships lives on in the compound formation of Swedish words for relatives, such as:

mor (mother) »	**mormor (maternal grandmother)** **literally mother's mother**
far (father) »	**farfar (paternal grandfather)** **literally father's father**
barn (child/children) »	**barnbarn (grandchildren)**

Brainteaser
From the above, can you work out what the Swedish words are for paternal grandmother and maternal grandfather?*

IT'S A FAMILY AFFAIR

Parental leave provisions in Sweden are among the most generous in the world, mothers and fathers having 480 days of paid leave per child to split between them, and single parents being given the option to take the whole lot! This, coupled with a foundation of child-centric social policies (in 1979, Sweden was the first nation in the world to ban the corporal punishment of children) means this is one family-oriented country.

No wonder then that the birthrate is increasing! In 2007, 107,421 babies were born in Sweden, the rate each year steadily rising thereafter, with a 'baby boom' increase of 7% on this figure in 2010, and 4% in 2011. So what are the names of all these newborns?

*farmor and morfar respectively

Most popular baby names in Sweden 2012

	GIRLS	BOYS
1.	Alice	William
2.	Elsa	Oscar
3.	Julia	Lucas
4.	Ella	Hugo
5.	Maja	Elias
6.	Ebba	Alexander
7.	Emma	Liam
8.	Linnea	Charlie
9.	Molly	Oliver
10.	Alva	Filip

Bucking the trend... Future Queen of Sweden, Princess Victoria and husband Prince Daniel gave their first child the rather untraditional name of Estelle in 2012

FIKA [fi:ka]
COFFEE BREAK

Say 'no' to a Swede's invitation to fika and you're saying 'no' to more than just a mug of the black stuff. Sweden is one of the world's biggest coffee-drinking nations (consuming in excess of 8 kg coffee per capita per annum) and its coffee breaks are a social ritual, part of the cultural fabric, and considered an essential tool for maintaining good relations and productivity in the workplace.

Speak the lingo: false friend

Many words can be confused in English and Swedish because they look like they mean the same thing. For example, if someone asks, "Vill du ha en kaka?" You might think they are asking if you'd like a cake, but in fact they're asking if you'd like a cookie or biscuit. To further fudge the issue, the concept of *mjuk kaka* exists, which does refer to cake, but only a 'soft' cake such as *morotskaka* (carrot cake) or *sockerkaka* (sponge cake). But if you really want your cake and eat it then you'd better order *tårta*, and *prinsesstårta* in particular, because that's the kind of cake fit for a princess!

You don't have to be a coffee-drinker to take part, however. The concept of fika encapsulates any short break with friends or colleagues, usually with something to eat. Here's what you might be offered:

BRYGGKAFFE/TE
A jug of Swedish *bryggkaffe* (drip-filtered coffee) is what you'll see sitting on hot plates in homes, offices, cafés… in fact, wherever you go. If it isn't fresh, it can be rather acidic, so you might prefer te (tea), available in as many varieties as you can dream up.

KAFFEBRÖD
Literally meaning 'coffee bread', *kaffebröd* is the collective term for the bakery delights designed to be eaten with your hot beverage, including *kanelbullar* (Swedish cinnamon buns) or *wienerlängd* (a large Danish pastry filled with créme pâtissière served in slices).

OSTMACKA
Your snack doesn't have to be sweet. Many Swedes opt for half a bread roll topped with cheese and a bit of greenery. *Ostmacka* is an office favourite.

Konditori – the classic Swedish cake shop

Why not skip the slick espresso atmosphere of the fashionable urban café for a more subdued fika experience at a traditional *konditori*? Along with your Swedish drip-filter coffee you may like to try:

RÄKMACKA

Plump pink prawns piled high on dark rye with sliced egg, mayo and lettuce make for a delicious and classic savoury treat.

PRINSESSTÅRTA

Swedes just love this vanilla, jam and whipped cream sponge encased in lurid green marzipan.

PUNSCHRULLAR

Also nicknamed *dammsugare* because they look like old-fashioned cylinder vacuum cleaners, these little marzipan rolls are made with the left-over crumbs from other cakes and flavoured with arrack liqueur.

*Café Tant Gredelin –
Enköping's cutest café
in one of its oldest
preserved buildings*

GULDGRUVA [gul:dgru:va]
GOLD MINE

It may not be the first country to spring to mind when it comes to gold prospecting but Sweden has a long history of mining its rich mineral deposits. Back in the 1920s, the region of Norrland experienced its first gold rush, when mines such as Boliden, near Skellefteå were established. In its 43 years as a working mine, 128 tonnes of gold were extracted, besides silver and other valuable products. Come the 21st Century, and gold fever has struck again with new discoveries along *Guldlinjen* (the 'Gold Line'), a regional tectonic zone stretching from the mountainous northwest of Västerbotten down to the Botnia coast. At a time when the price of gold just keeps on soaring, this is welcome news for a sparsely populated and economically depressed area.

Gold digger's delight

SVARTLIDEN
This open pit mine owned by Dragon Mining was brought into production in 2005. By the end of March 2012 it had produced 292,475 ounces of gold – that's over 8 metric tonnes!

STORKULLEN
After chancing upon a gold deposit while looking for blueberries in 2007, two amateur mineral hunters, Harriet Svensson and Siv Wiik, sold their high-grade mining prospect to a Canadian firm for SEK 21 million.

BJÖRKDAL
All that glitters here really is gold – the mine being unique in Sweden with visible gold-bearing quartz veins. Approximately 1 tonne of pure gold is extracted at Björkdal each year – around 20% of Sweden's total annual gold production.

Of course, steel is the metal upon which Swedes have built a reputation, the mighty SSAB at the forefront with a crude steel production capacity of 6 million tonnes. Indeed, an affinity for iron really is in the blood, as high grade steel has been produced in Sweden ever since the Viking Age. But there's a bit more than ferrous oxide in the bedrock of the nation:

STORA KOPPARBERGET
Named a UNESCO world heritage site in 2001, the ancient copper mine in Falun operated for a millennium from the 10th Century to 1992 and was for hundreds of years the most important industrial site in the country. New copper prospects are being found around Sweden all the time but are unlikely to surpass the reputation of the 'Great Copper Mountain'.

RARE EARTH ON RESARÖ
The Ytterby mine on the island of Resarö just 20km outside Stockholm well deserves its reputation as home of the rare earths (REEs) since seven in the series of seventeen elements were discovered there in the 19th Century. Vital to new technologies from iPhones to MRI machines, REEs continue to be prospected in Sweden and elsewhere.

Speak the lingo: Mind your Metal!

STÅLMANNEN
Yes, 'Steelman' is Swedish for Superman – not surprising really…

GRUVA
By name, perhaps not by nature…While the noun *gruva* means 'mine', the reflexive verb 'att gruva sig' means to dread or be anxious.

NORRLANDS GULD
Not just the literal 'gold of Norrland' but a famous Swedish lager too.

A typical Swedish farmhouse painted with the famous Falu rödfärg, a traditional red pigment rich in wood-preserving minerals from the Falun copper mines

Stora Kopparberget, the most important industrial site in Sweden for centuries

HALKA [hal:ka]
SLIP/SLIDE

Anyone taking their driving licence in Sweden will be in for an extra thrill – the *halkbana*, a car skid-training track designed to give you an 'out of control' experience you won't forget! Such training is a useful exercise, however, in a country that endures dangerous, icy conditions on the roads for a good few months of the year.

It can start as early as October, the first frosts prompting Swedes to consider changing their tyres to *vinterdäck* (winter tyres) that provide better road grip, with or without studs. Come 1st December, these become compulsory kit if the local police determine that winter conditions prevail. Since this can vary considerably from north to south, and through the season, most people just leave their winter tyres on until 31st March, which is the end of the mandatory period.

THE ONLY WAY TO ENJOY A SWEDISH WINTER IS TO WRAP UP WELL! LOOK HOW COLD IT CAN GET:

Average minimum temperatures	Jan	Feb	March
Kiruna	-19	-18	-14
Östersund	-10	-9	-6
Stockholm	-5	-5	-3

Don't slip up!
If you're planning on taking your own car to Sweden in the winter, you will need winter tyres too! Foreign registered vehicles are NOT exempt from the regulation. Check your tyres are marked M+S (mud + snow).

Speak the lingo
Trying to explain something complicated and getting into deep water? If a Swede thinks your argument doesn't hold up, they might say: "Nu är du ute på hal is" (lit. you're on slippery ice now), idiomatically equivalent to: "you're on thin ice/shaky ground there".

THE SLIPPERY SLOPE TO WINTER-SPORTS HEAVEN

Of course, sliding around on snow and ice can be bags of fun too, if you're into…

SLEDGING
Most parks in Sweden will be landscaped with some kind of hill, ready for winter-time tobogganing exploits. If that sounds too tame, you could always try dog-sledging in the wilds of Lapland.

ICE SKATING
In winter, public football pitches transform into ice-rinks, so everyone can perfect their pirouettes or ice-hockey tackles free of charge. For more of a challenge, take up *långfärdsskriskoåkning* – long-distance skating on lakes or archipelago waters when the natural ice is safe.

DOWNHILL SKIING/SNOWBOARDING
They may not compare with the Alpine greats of France or Switzerland but Sweden's many small ski resorts are family-friendly and very accessible. Åre in Jämtland provides the best all-round experience, while Riksgränsen in Lapland is the most exotic, with skiing opportunities as late into the year as midsummer.

CROSS-COUNTRY SKIING
Your winter fitness is guaranteed with regular cross-country skiing, which demands strength, skill and stamina. Miles of *elljusspår* (artificially lit tracks) over snow-clad forest terrain will keep you going as darkness descends. NB, for the best snow conditions head inland and north of Stockholm.

Riksgränsen

IDROTT [i:drot:]
PHYSICAL SPORT

If sport is as old as the hills then so is *idrott*, the Swedish word for physical sport, derived from the Old Norse ið (activity) and þróttr (strength or endurance). And the emphasis is on the physical because even though the English word sport is widely used synonymously, only idrott refers to sports in which an individual's physical skill and strength is the main focus.

Ever since the dawn of the modern Olympics, Sweden has emerged as a nation producing idrottare of exceptional ability – sportsmen and women proving themselves in track and field, on the ski slopes or on the ball court.

Zlatan Ibrahimović, seven-time winner of the Swedish Guldbollen prize for best male Swedish football player, has made his mark as a top international sports star

SWEDISH SPORTS STARS KEEP ON SHINING

When the newspaper, Dagens Nyheter compiled its list of the 100 greatest sportsmen and women of the last hundred years in 1999, tennis prodigy Björn Borg came in at number 23, and slalom legend, Ingemar Stenmark at number 47. Since then, new generations of Swedish stars have lit up the international scene.

NHL – AN ELITE ARENA

Sweden may be holding its head high in world-class handball and football, but it has ice hockey to thank for its greatest international fame and fortune. And it is through the American National Hockey League that many of Sweden's world champion players have achieved stardom.

Håkan Loob, Börje Salming, Markus Näslund, Mats Sundin and Peter Forsberg are just a handful of the top Swedish ice hockey players to grace the NHL throughout recent history – Alexander Steen, Henrik Zetterberg and Johan Franzén are a few of the new ones making it big time.

Golden oldies' Ingemar Stenmark (skiing), Ulrika Knape (diving) and Björn Borg (tennis) posing with an exercise bike in Stockholm 1974

ALPINE EVENTS

SLALOM AND SUPER G
The incredible Olympic gold talents of Pernilla Wiberg and Anja Pärson are hard acts to follow, both women also winning strings of World Championships, Wiberg in the 1990s and Pärson in the 2000s.

SNOWBOARDING
Since Jan Boklöv revolutionised ski-jumping with his V-style in the early 1990s, a number of Swedes have soared to new heights – this time on the snowboard – record-breaking Ingemar Backman and Johan Olofsson among them.

CROSS-COUNTRY
Gunde Svan and Thomas Wassberg became national heroes in the 1980s after each winning four Olympic gold medals in their respective distances. The strong tradition of this sport in Sweden continues, with stars such as three-time Vasaloppet winners, Daniel Tynell (2002, 2006, 2009) and Jörgen Brink (2010, 2011, 2012).

Names to watch: Jon Olsson freestyler (qualified for 2014 Olympics)

TRACK AND FIELD

HIGH JUMP
Following in the footsteps of former world record holder, Patrik Sjöberg, Kajsa Bergqvist and Stefan Holm have both enjoyed record-breaking success, winning Olympic bronze in 2000 (Bergqvist) and Olympic gold in 2004 (Holm), as well as numerous World and European Championship golds and silvers during the early 2000s.

HEPTATHLON
The title of all-round super athlete must go to three-time World and double European heptathlon champion, Carolina Klüft, who also clinched an Olympic gold at Athens in 2004. She is the only athlete ever to win three world titles in heptathlon (2003, 2005 and 2007).

TRIPLE JUMP
Also a high jumper, Christian Olsson is better known for his triple jump, having won three World and two European Championships between 2003-2006 and Olympic gold in 2004.

Names to watch: Lisa Nordén (Women's triathlon Olympic silver 2012)

Lisa Nordén in training. She has recently won a number of prestigious sports awards, including the 2013 title of Swedish Female Athlete of the Year

JUL [jul]
CHRISTMAS

If you're dreaming of a white Christmas, then Sweden is a great place to be, with postcard-perfect settings for a traditional . Indeed, as the etymology of the Old English word, 'Yule' would hint, many of our modern Christmas customs are of Nordic origin. So for a really authentic feel to one of the biggest celebrations of the year, do it the Swedish way!

NU ÄR DET JUL IGEN...

For Swedes, *juletiden* implies all the usual elements of over-indulgence and family entertainment, but with a mixture of traditions.

Here's what you need to go Swedish at Xmas:

SET THE DATE
Like many other European countries, Sweden has its actual Christmas celebrations on Christmas Eve – *julafton*.

DECORATE YOUR TREE WITH GOATS
One of the oldest Swedish Christmas symbols is *julbocken* (the Yule goat), dating back to pre-Christian times and associated with the Norse god Thor. As precursor to *jultomten* (Santa Claus), *julbocken* was once the Christmas gift-bearer but has now been reduced to a straw figure, often used as a Christmas tree decoration.

PREPARE WITH PEPPARKAKOR
The countdown to Christmas would not be the same without *glögg* and *pepparkakor* parties to bring on some festive cheer. In Sweden, a variety of spiced wines and gingerbread can be bought for the occasion, or try your hand at making your own.

DITCH THE TURKEY
Julskinka (Christmas ham) is the centre piece of the smorgasbord, which also includes an array of pickled herring, meatballs, cheeses, rye breads and more.

...AND SING SILLY SONGS!
Nothing new there but you might like to learn Swedish ones such as, *Nu är det jul igen*! (Christmas is here again) and *Bjällerklang* (Jingle Bells). Look up www.julsanger.net for a selection of songs and lyrics!

A WHOLE YEAR OF
SWEDISH CELEBRATIONS

From the New Year onwards, visitors to Sweden may be flummoxed by a whole host of celebrations with a uniquely Swedish take. Here are just three of them:

FETTISDAG
Shrove Tuesday was originally celebrated with the eating of buns to mark the start of Lent. Now the months between Christmas and Easter are one big bun fight, as Swedish bakeries vie to create the best *semla* – the cardamom bun filled with almond paste and whipped cream that Swedes go mad for.

VALBORGSMÄSSOAFTON
The night of Walpurgis Eve (30th April) is lit up with the blaze of bonfires as households have a good old clear out and celebrate the start of spring – a custom dating back to medieval times and the cult of Saint Walpurga.

MIDSOMMAR
No-one escapes Midsummer celebrations in Sweden, as the whole nation practically closes down in the third week of June and heads off to the countryside to revel in the summer solstice.

Folk dancing in traditional costume – a classic scene from Midsummer festivities

KARTA [ka:ta]
MAP

Flying into Arlanda, it may strike you that you are descending into a vast expanse of rural evergreen, not the urban capital of Stockholm. Indeed, roughly 53% of Sweden's 450,000 km² land area is forest, most Swedes preferring to settle in or around one of the ten largest cities in the southern half of the country. This is no terrible squeeze, however, as the entire population is a tiny 9.5 million.

So, lots of space for everyone – but where's it all at?

1. STOCKHOLM
The magnetic pull of the capital means there are around 2 million people living in and around the city, which also welcomes over a million tourists each year.

2. GOTHENBURG
The epicurean epicentre of Scandinavia is home to approximately a million inhabitants in the city and its environs.

3. MALMÖ
Gateway to the continent via the Öresund bridge, this important city has a population of around half a million, including the greater Malmö area.

Stortorget (The Great Square) in Stockholm Old Town, current home of the Swedish Academy and Nobel Museum but historically the scene of mass slaughter during the Stockholm blood bath of 1520 in an age of vicious fighting over Swedish sovereignty

...And other significant, albeit smaller centres in Sweden:

UPPSALA AND LUND
These two cities enjoy academic cudos as revered seats of learning – Uppsala university (est. 1477) is the oldest centre of higher education in Scandinavia and Lund university (est. 1666) one of the largest.

ÖREBRO
Situated in the heart of the country, Örebro is the logistical hub of Sweden, with one of the fastest growing urban populations in the country. Örebro airport is becoming increasingly important for business and leisure.

UMEÅ
Björkarnas stad ('City of Birches') on the Botnia coast, is something of a cultural centre for the north of Sweden. It is also thriving as a university town, and home to many cutting-edge science and research companies.

KIRUNA
The clear skies of the arctic circle are one of Kiruna's attractions, as home to the ESTRACK tracking station and Space tech community, SSC. The economy of Kiruna has largely been centred around the mining of iron ore, but tourism is becoming increasingly important.

Left: Death metal band, Death Maze performing at the Kulturnatta festival, Umeå, 21st May 2011

Above: The imposing Örebro castle, surrounded by a moat

Above right: Kiruna – a city actually on the move, due to expansion of the mine

Right: Adelgatan in the cultural quarter of Lund

LJUS [ju:s]
LIGHT

In a land of luminous extremes from the whitest of nights to the darkest of days, an obsession with light can only be the cultural norm. For Swedes, this obsession is reflected in everything from interior design to seasonal habits: nowhere like the North reminds us of how dependent we are on sunlight for our health, our happiness and ultimately, our survival.

LIGHT FANTASTIC

AT HOME

Pale pine floors and minimalistic white-washed walls are the hallmarks of a Swedish interior, maximizing light and space indoors. A colourful cushion or two are never far away though, and don't forget the whole treasure chest full of candles – ready to brighten up those bare windows as the nights grow longer.

OUTDOORS

If you can't flood your home with natural sunlight, better go outside then. No matter what the air temperature, when the sun comes out, so do the people. Alfresco dining in mid February? With heat lamps on the decking and a bundle of blankets, anything is possible!

ONGOING INNOVATION

Growing interest in the effects of light on psychological and physical health has stimulated a demand for lighting planners and designers with the skills to create esthetic and technically advanced lighting solutions for both private and public environments. Jönköping university's degree programme in light design is at the cutting edge.

OVERDOSE ON THE LIGHT STUFF AT...

ALLHELGONA
All Saints Day (falling between 31st October and 6th November) literally sees Sweden glow, as many pay their respects to the dead with a beautiful and heart-warming abundance of candlelight.

LUCIA
The run up to the winter solstice and Christmas would not be the same without celebrating Saint Lucia on 13th December, every church and school crammed full of girls wearing candle crowns and white gowns.

MIDSOMMAR
Raise a glass or three to the summer solstice and enjoy a little Midsummer madness in the third week of June, as 24-hour daylight goes to your head. Verdant surroundings and the freshest of early summer produce make it the nation's favourite time of year.

As spooky and unreal as it may appear, norrsken (Aurora Borealis) is a most natural atmospheric phenomenon. Caused by the collision of charged particles with atoms in the high-altitude atmosphere, the aurora is often displayed as curtains of fluorescent green that can change in seconds or glow steadily for hours, depending on conditions. Normally most visible in winter at the high latitudes of northern Sweden, auroral zones can expand to lower latitudes under the influence of geomagnetic disturbances, allowing more of the country to experience norrsken, as it did early in 2012 after a solar storm

MATKORG [ma:tkorj]
FOOD BASKET

Despite the ubiquity of global brands and familiar packaging, supermarkets in foreign supermarkets can still surprise and delight with curious local products, and Swedish ones are no exception.

Buying groceries and preparing your own food on your visit rather than eating out all the time will add authenticity to your cultural experience, and, considering the price of restaurants in Sweden, will also save you a lot of cash. So, what Swedish staples should you put in your basket?

Dagens – your best value lunchtime deal

Eating out can be relatively painless on the purse if you do it at lunchtime, which in Sweden is usually between 11.30am-12.30pm. Scores of restaurants compete for business with all-inclusive deals, and for around SEK 100 you can get a hot main, salad, cold drink, coffee and biscuits. *Dagens* (dish of the day) will be priced a little lower than the other options on the *matsedel* (menu).

BRÖD

Hard or soft? is just one of many questions you may ask yourself, when confronted with the array of Swedish breads on offer, for example:

KNÄCKEBRÖD

Crispbread, usually made from rye or a combination of grains – a must-have in any Swedish home.

TUNNBRÖD

'Thin bread' that can be hard or soft and made from wheat, barley and rye. Soft *tunnbröd* is popular and convenient for making sandwich wraps.

LIMPA

A soft rye loaf that can be light or dark and gains its texture and sweetness from syrup.

OST
Västerbotten, *Grevé*, and *Svarta Sara* are three of the stronger flavoured, firm cheeses you will encounter. Equip yourself with a traditional osthyvel (cheese slicer) to make light work of open-sandwich preparation.

KALLES KAVIAR
Swedes abroad get homesick for this salty, pink cod-roe paste and wouldn't dream of having a cheese or egg sandwich without it!

FILMJÖLK/GRÄDDFIL
Cartons of these cultured dairy products look much the same as those for ordinary milk, so beware! You may want to try *filmjölk* (sour milk) with your cereal and *gräddfil* (soured cream) as a dip with nachos.

FALUKORV
Immediately recognisable by its bright red skin, *falukorv* is a large pork and beef sausage and a family favourite in Sweden. Throw it into pasta, bake it whole or use it for *korv stroganoff* – its versatility knows no bounds.

INLAGD SILL
Everyone has heard of pickled herring but you may not realise just how many types there are until you see them in a Swedish supermarket – onion, dill, mustard, garlic…the list goes on.

NOBEL [nobæl:]
NOBEL

It may seem a bitter irony that the man who made his fortune from developing arms and explosives would later relinquish it all in the interests of world peace. But when Alfred Nobel invented dynamite in 1867 he could not fully comprehend how it would impact on the course of human history.

As a young chemical engineer, Nobel became very interested in nitro-glycerine and its practical applications in construction work, and it was only once he had found a way to stabilize the compound and manage it safely that the full-blown power of dynamite became obvious to a war-mongering world.

EXPLOSIVE MIND, PACIFIST NATURE

Nobel was not only a gifted inventor but also...

- An exceptionally talented linguist, fluent in Swedish, Russian, French, English and German by the age of 17. He taught himself French by translating Voltaire into Swedish and then back into French, checking it against the original.

- Greatly interested in literature and wrote his own poetry and dramatic works. Among Nobel's favourite authors were Byron, Tolstoy and Ibsen.

- Took an active interest in social and peace-related issues, and was clearly influenced over the years by his friend, Bertha von Suttner, who became a prominent figure in the peace movement.

THE PRIZE OF A LIFETIME

Alfred Nobel had the rare and ominous opportunity to read his own obituary in 1888 after a French newspaper erroneously reported his death when in fact it was his brother Ludwig who had passed away. Sentiments expressed in the obituary such as 'the merchant of death is dead', are said to have disappointed Nobel and prompted him to leave a more honourable legacy – that of the Nobel Prizes.

- Upon his death in 1896, Nobel left 94% of his total assets (SEK 31,225,000) to establish the five Nobel Prizes, now worth around SEK 3.1 billion or EUR 337 million.

- The Nobel Prize has been awarded almost every year since 1901 for achievements in physics, chemistry, physiology or medicine, literature and for peace. The Prize for Economic Sciences was established by the National Bank of Sweden in 1968.

- Prizes can be awarded to one person, shared between 2 or 3 individuals, or even awarded to whole organisations. The Nobel Peace Prize, for example, has been awarded to Amnesty International (1977), Médecins sans Frontières (1999) and the EU (2012).

- Each year, the specialist committee for each subject sends out thousands of invitations to field experts around the world to nominate Nobel Prize candidates for the coming year. The selection committees for each subject prize are all connected to distinguished academic bodies in Sweden (for example, the Swedish Academy of Sciences) with the exception of the Peace Prize, which is awarded by the Norwegian Nobel Committee in Oslo.

The magnificent Nobel Awards Ceremony and banquet take place on 10th December each year in Stockholm. Left: a bird's eye view of the 2012 ceremony at the Stockholm Concert Hall

ORDBOK [o:dbok]
DICTIONARY

Part of the fun of travelling is listening to other peoples' conversations in a foreign language and trying to work out whether they are revealing some world-shattering secret or just telling someone what they had for lunch. Whatever the intrigue, however, it always helps to have some insider information, so here's your heads-up on Swedish!

GET TO GRIPS WITH THE BASICS

Basic Swedish grammar is easy to learn, with no verb conjugation based on person or number, or any complicated case system to worry about. For example:

Subject: Jag/han/hon/du/vi/de   Present tense verb: äter   Object: glass

    I/he/she/you/we/they   eat(s) OR am/is/are eating   ice-cream

EXPLOIT YOUR NATURAL ASSETS

Your chances of decoding a conversation in Swedish will be greatly improved if you know another Germanic language. Don't get caught out by apparent similarities, though, as there are many 'false friends'! Test yourself with this quick quiz:

TRANSLATE THE FOLLOWING SWEDISH WORDS INTO ENGLISH:

1. koka   **2. gå**   **3. chef**   **4. vrist**   **5. aktuell**

Answers: 1. boil not cook   2. walk in the first instance, then go, but not always as in English 3. boss/manager not chef 4. ankle not wrist 5. current/topical not actual

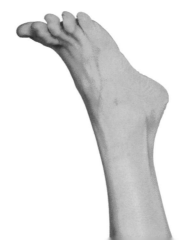

KEEP UP WITH COLLOQUIALISMS

Spoken Swedish sometimes departs quite significantly from its full written form, occasionally omitting verbs or subjects altogether! Learn to recognize short forms and colloquialisms, for example:

YOU HEAR	FULL 'CORRECT' VERSION	MEANING
Läget?	Hur är läget?	How's it going?
Han ba/han sa ba...	Han sade bara...	He just said...
Han e på toa/muggen	Han är på toaletten	He's in the loo/john
Ska du me?	Skall du följa med?	Are you coming (with me/us)?
Ses!	Vi ses!	See you!

THE ART OF SAYING HELLO...

Saying hello in Swedish isn't as straightforward as you might think! Generally, you can't go wrong by saying *hej*, which is the most common and universally accepted greeting in formal and informal settings. The variations on this and other greetings are many, however, and depend on context:

HEJ, HEJ!

The double form is friendlier than a single *Hej*! and commonly used when entering an apparently empty room or a shop, in order to attract attention.

HEJSAN!

Slightly more informal/friendlier than *Hej*! and perhaps best used with people you know.

TJENARE!/TJENA!/TJA!

All three forms of this colloquial greeting are used to varying degrees, depending on context and who is being addressed. It's quite 'matey' in tone, the shortest form *Tja*! being preferred by young males!

HALLÅ

This can often sound rather abrupt and strange. Swedes may use it to answer the phone or as a question to check you're still on the line if the connection is bad. It also serves as attention-grabber in the rather brusque phrase, *Men hallå där!* to point something out, especially if you've done something wrong!

GOD MORGON/GOD DAG/GOD KVÄLL/GOD NATT

God dag and *god kväll* are polite greetings generally only heard when Swedes want to be formal, which isn't often! By all means say *god morgon* to the first people you meet when you wake up, however, and *god natt* to the last people you see at night!

POLARPRISET [pola:rprisæt]
THE POLAR MUSIC PRIZE

No encyclopedia of Sweden would be complete without some mention of ABBA, the pop group that became one of the most commercially successful musical acts of all time. But in the spotlight here is their manager, Stig 'Stikkan' Anderson, as founder of the most prestigious international music award, The Polar Music Prize.

After a hugely successful career as composer and lyrics writer for a number of artists under his record label, Polar Music, Anderson decided to donate SEK 42 million to establish 'the world's biggest music prize'. His dream came true in 1992 when the prize was awarded for the first time.

The colourful Icelandic artist, Björk

TWENTY YEARS OF WINNING MUSICIANS

Awarded for "significant achievements in music and/or musical activity" or "of great potential importance for music or musical activity", the Polar Music Prize is not determined by jury but by a committee of music industry professionals. Each year, winners are awarded SEK 1 million. Famous names to have clinched the prize over the past twenty years include:

1992 Paul McCartney, the singer/songwriter
"for his creativity and imagination as a composer and artist which has revitalized popular music worldwide over the last 30 years."

1998 Ravi Shankar, the legendary sitar player
"for nearly six decades of achievement as a brilliant performer and explorer of his country's art music".

2006 Led Zeppelin, the rock band
for being "one of the great pioneers of rock", the "mysticism and primal energy" of their experimental music having "come to define the genre 'hard rock'".

2010 Björk, the avant-garde Icelandic artist
for "her deeply personal music and lyrics, her precise arrangements and her unique voice..."

2012 Yo-Yo Ma, the leading cellist of our time
for dedicating "his virtuosity and his heart to journeys of musical exploration and discovery around the world".

Yo-Yo Ma,
virtuoso cellist

AFTER ABBA, SWEDISH POP STAYS ON TOP

Roxette, The Cardigans, Robyn, Swedish House Mafia… the post ABBA years have been filled with Swedish music successes. Here are some of the new kids on the block:

LYKKE LI
This indie pop cutie had international success with the hit 'Little Bit' from her debut album *Youth Novels* in 2008 and continues to be just a 'little bit' cool. The New York Times named Lykke Li's second album, *Wounded Rhymes* eighth best album of 2011 and the singer won best artist and best album award at the 2012 Swedish Grammis.

FIRST AID KIT
After the release of their debut album, *The Big Black & The Blue* in 2010, The folksy sister duo from Stockholm went on an extensive tour of the USA, Canada, Australia, New Zealand and parts of Europe. Their second album, *The Lion's Roar* went straight to no.1 in Sweden when it was released in January 2012 and reached no.35 in the UK.

THE KNIFE
The electronic music duo from Gothenburg gained international recognition with their albums *Deep Cuts* (2003) and *Silent Shout* (2006) and have won a number of Swedish Grammis but generally stay shy of the media and refuse to attend awards ceremonies. Their next album, *Shaking the Habitual* is to be released in 2013.

AND NOT FORGETTING THE SWEDISH DJS FOLLOWING IN ERIC PRYDZ' FOOTSTEPS:
Avicii (Levels, 2011) and Adrian Lux (Teenage Crime 2010).

Avicii in action

The First Aid Kit sisters

Q-MÄRKNING [kumærkning]
Q-LISTING

Like many other European countries keen to preserve their heritage, Sweden is active in protecting its historic and culturally significant buildings and sites known as *byggnadsminnen*. These range from an impressive number of world heritage sites including medieval castles and historic industrial centres to less imposing but equally fascinating art nouveau cinemas and modernist villas.

The system in place to preserve sites like these is known as *Q-märkning,* a legally more robust designation than the former *K-märkning* (*kulturmärkning*) for places of cultural and historic importance. So whether your interest is Viking remains or 20th Century architecture, there are pieces of Sweden left intact through the ages to amaze and inspire you.

Q is for quirky
Can a radio station be classified as a cultural treasure? In Sweden, yes! Having formed part of a worldwide network of long wave stations in commercial use from the 1920s, Grimeton Radio Station in Varberg is the only surviving example of a major transmitting station based on pre-electronic technology. Grimeton became a World Heritage Site in 2004.

Grimeton with antenna towers

Q'D UP FROM NORTH TO SOUTH

GAMMELSTADS KYRKSTAD, LULEÅ

Granted UNESCO World Heritage status in 1995, the cluster of 424 wooden houses surrounding an early 15th Century stone church is the best-preserved example of a 'church village' – a unique type of village once found in northern Scandinavia. It was only used on Sundays and at religious festivals to accommodate worshippers from afar who could not return home the same day because of difficult travelling conditions.

TANUM, BOHUSLÄN

The Bronze Age rock art here is unique compared to that found in other parts of the world due to its exceptional artistic quality. Over 500 rock carving sites exist in the area, with tens of thousands of pictures creating complex and vivid scene depictions of the every day life, warfare and religion of the ancients.

GOTLAND

Around 360 *byggnadsminnen* make the whole of Gotland a historian's dream, from the atmospheric medieval buildings of Visby to the charmingly preserved farmyards and stone cottages of the Gotland countryside. Neighbouring Fårö is also an area of outstanding natural beauty and home to the 1,000 year-old Ava oak tree.

AND FAIRY TALE CASTLES DOTTED HERE, THERE AND EVERYWHERE...

The magnificent Drottningholm (Stockholm), Läckö slott (Lake Vänern, South) and Borgholm (Öland) are just three of Sweden's many castles and palaces standing witness to a long history of wealth, world-dealings and warfare.

Above left: The city wall of Visby, Gotland, dating from the 13th Century

Above right: rock carvings at Tanum

Bottom left: Gammelstads 'church village', Luleå

Bottom right: Drottningholm palace, Stockholm

REN [re:n]
REINDEER

While Santa's reindeer might fly through the air to the sound of Jingle Bells, most Swedish reindeer have distinctly earth-bound lives as herd animals to the Sámi, the indigenous peoples of Sápmi (Lapland). Reindeer roam and are managed over a vast area in Sweden's northernmost reaches – an area representing about a third of the country, from Idre in the south to Treriksröset in the north.

Reindeer husbandry has been at the heart of Sámi culture for centuries but few individuals now earn a living from it. Of the approximately 20,000 Sámi who live in Sweden (Sápmi also extends over Norway, Finland and Russia) only 2,500 are active in herding reindeer and almost all of these additionally work in other sectors such as tourism, construction and mining.

Take life by the horns...
• To live off reindeer, a herder must have at least 400 animals – very few Sámi have this many.

• Until about 1950, reindeer herding was done on skis, with reindeer dogs to control and move the herd. Since then, technology has completely revolutionised the process, and snowmobiles, helicopters and satellite communications all now assist the fast movement of animals across long distances.

• A *sameby* is a reindeer-herding community and also the geographical area in which they may manage their animals.

R

Rangifer Tarandus et al.

There are several types of reindeer native to the arctic tundras and sub-arctic woodlands of the Northern Hemisphere, including the caribou of North America. Reindeer are the only type of deer to have been domesticated on a large scale – a phenomenon among arctic peoples that is believed to have started as early as the Bronze or Iron Age.

Reindeer have seasonally adaptable feet: when the tundra is soft and wet in the summer, their footpads become sponge-like and provide extra traction. As winter approaches, the pads shrink and tighten, revealing the rim of their hooves, which help cut into the ice and crusted snow to keep the reindeer from slipping.

All that roaming and a healthy diet of lichen and tender birch leaves means reindeer are prized for their meat, which is rich, lean and high in nutritional value. Try delicious roast *rensadel* (reindeer saddle) for a celebratory dinner or pan-fried *renskav* (thin slices) with mashed potato for a weekday treat.

OTHER FURRY NATIVES:
WOLF, BEAR AND MOOSE ON THE LOOSE

- Although wolves became extinct in Sweden in the 1970s, they began to re-appear almost a decade later, having crossed over from Finland and Russia. Protection has helped numbers grow, especially in central Sweden, and the wolf population now stands at around 200.

- They make for an unusual sighting but brown bears are thriving in Swedish forests, such as those in Dalarna. The Swedish bear population was estimated to be around 3,000 in 2004.

- Whether you prefer to call them moose or elk, these 'kings of the forest' can be found all over Sweden – occasionally making a nuisance of themselves in people's gardens. Weighing in at up to a hefty half tonne, moose are best approached with caution, although rarely dangerous.

S

SYSTEMBOLAGET [systembola:gæt]
SYSTEMBOLAGET

A national institution with over 150 years in the running, the Swedish alcohol monopoly may seem like an anachronism in a modern, free-trade environment. However, when Sweden became a member of the EU in 1994, it was anxious to protect its alcohol policy and subsequently won the right to retain *Systembolaget*.

Despite generous alcohol import allowances within the European community, *Systembolaget* remains popular with Swedes, partly due to its impressive range of products and high levels of expertise and service but most importantly because of its role in promoting public awareness of alcohol and health issues.

THE PROBLEM WITH POTATOES...

Why did *Systembolaget* start in the first place? Because of the potato! Here's how:

1746 Potatoes were used to make *brännvin* (aquavit) in Sweden for the first time, but no-one had yet had the bright idea to eat them! *Brännvin* had been made from grain until now, but that was needed for making bread. Potatoes were a very cheap alternative.

1829 The Swedish population, kids included, were now drinking 46 litres of brännvin per year. Admittedly, this spirituosa wasn't as strong as its modern equivalent, but still...

1850 A few quarrymen from Falun established the first *Systembolaget* in the interests of 'morality'. Profits were used for the benefit of the general public.

And after that... The concept of *Systembolaget* took off and by 1905 all brännvin in the country was sold by special state-controlled companies. In the post WWI decades, while the USA went for prohibition, Sweden chose the 'less extreme' route of strict regulation, issuing a special alcohol rations book – *motboken*. In years to come, this would be scrapped and alcohol policy refined but *Systembolaget's* objective is still the same: 'To minimize alcohol-related problems by selling alcohol in a responsible way, without profit motive.'

Snaps was born to complement pickled herring and boiled potatoes

Speak the lingo: Skall du på Bolaget?

When Swedes talk about going to Systembolaget they often ab-
breviate the name to *'Systemet'* or *'Bolaget'*. This can be confus-
ing as the words in isolation mean 'system' and 'company' respectively. So if someone asks you, *"Skall du på Bolaget?"* they'll
be wondering if you're going to buy drinks, not if you're going
to work! And if you end up being sent away with their shopping
list, here's what you should know:

• Systembolaget sells *starköl* (beers exceeding 3.5% alc./vol),
  wine, spirits, cider and alcohol-free drinks. For beers such as
  folköl (max 3.5% alc./vol) and *lättöl* (max 2.2% alc./vol), go
  to the supermarket, where beers and ciders with low alcohol
  content are legally sold.

• If the cashier asks, *"Har du leg?"* they are not asking you to
  bare your ankles, they are asking for ID! You have to be over
  the age of 20 to purchase alcohol at *Systembolaget*.

• *Systembolaget* is never open at night or on a Sunday. *Öppet-
  tider* (opening times) are generally between 10-18.00 on week-
  days and 10-13.00 on Saturdays.

TANTALISING TIPPLES TO WARM YOUR COCKLES

Clever advertising has made Absolut a household name but Sweden produces more than just this famous 'fire water':

BEER
Traditional big name lagers such as Åbro and Mariestads are ever-popular but there is now a huge selection of small-brewery niche offerings from pale ales and wheat beers to chocolatey stouts.

CIDER
Swedish fruit-flavoured ciders have recently taken the international market by storm. You may have heard of Rekorderlig and Kopparberg ciders.

SNAPS
Flavoured aquavit is something of a Swedish speciality. Hallands fläder and OP Andersson are just two of the many subtle concoctions you might like to try.

TRÄ [træ:]
WOOD

Ever tasted bark bread or sampled birch sap? Slept in a tree house or learnt how to timber a hut? Experiencing the wonders of wood is easy where trees are in the life-blood of the country.

Sweden ranks among the top world exporters of sawn wood products, pulp and paper but forestry here means so much more than maximising profit from a natural resource, it is also about sustainability, protecting bio-diversity and promoting appreciation for all aspects of the forest environment. Urnatur wood hermitage in the province of Östergötland and Kolarbyn eco-lodge in Västmanland are two examples of prize-winning enter-prises focused on these very aspects and offering people the chance to get back to nature – whether that means experiencing a night in a simple wooden hut without electricity or learning how to forage wild herbs for food. Wherever you are in Sweden, though, you'll never be far from a forest of adventures.

KNOW YOUR WOOD...

GRAN
The Swedish stock standard, spruce is the conifer of choice for Christmas. Luckily, no-one got their woolly mitts on a particular big beauty from the province of Dalarna, which at the age of 9,550 years is the world's oldest recorded tree.

TALL/FURU
Pine can be immediately distinguished from spruce by its bare trunk, with branches emanating higher up the tree. Being harder and more resinous than spruce, pine makes for a more versatile and durable timber and is heavily employed in the construction industry.

Kåda (resin) from spruce and pine has a long history of use for its antiseptic and skin-healing properties. The needles and young shoots from both trees also have high vitamin C content and can be eaten fresh or boiled to make tea.

BJÖRK
Birch is the most common deciduous tree in Sweden and a great friend in need, as its branches make excellent firewood, even when fresh off the tree in freezing conditions. Birch sap is traditionally extracted to make an edible syrup, and is increasingly in demand as a source of xylitol – a natural sugar substitute.

BAKE YOUR BARK...

In historic times of famine in Scandinavia, bark meal was mixed with rye and wheat flour to make bread. As it turned out, bark meal contains more zinc, magnesium and iron than rye and wheat and is full of fibre, so bark bread was a nutritional godsend. In modern times, the virtues of 'woody' bread have been rediscovered, so make sure you try it next time you're in Sweden!

A classic chair design,
Norrgavel

Decorative cupboard,
Svenskt Tenn

Släden,
Carl Malmsten

FASHION YOUR FURNITURE...

Träslöjd Woodwork is a long-established part of the school curriculum in Sweden and enthusiasts can continue to hone their craft at the numerous *folkhögskolor* (folk high-schools) which often specialise in arts and crafts subjects. Famous woodwork hot spots include the northern provinces of Dalarna and Norrbotten. But if admiring someone else's handiwork is more your style, you can always purchase a fine piece of wooden furniture from a Swedish company such as Norrgavel, Carl Malmsten or Svenskt Tenn.

UNDERHÅLLNING [undærhol:ning]
ENTERTAINMENT

When they're not packing a rucksack for an impromptu skating trip or lakeside barbecue, Swedes enjoy a bit of classic entertainment just like the rest of us. From a cosy night in with a good movie to a special night out at a star-studded show, there is plenty of home-grown fun to be had.

FILM

Greta Garbo and Ingrid Bergman may have been immortalized by Hollywood but Pinewood has a penchant for Swedes too, with five Swedish actresses stepping into the role of Bond girl over the years. One of these, Maud Adams, was definitely up to 007 standard, as she appeared twice, first with Britt Ekland in *The Man with the Golden Gun* (1974) and then in the title role of *Octopussy* (1983) along with Kristina Wayborn. Since Britt and Kristina are also Swedish, it was a double whammy all round!

Greta Garbo, whose mysterious allure holds an enduring fascination

SHOWS

Renowned illusionist and three-time recipient of the Merlin Award, Joe Labero is one of the world's biggest magicians. His busy international schedule means you probably won't get to see him live in Stockholm, but his amazing shows are a once-in-a-lifetime experience so catch one of his world tour dates if you can! Fellow Swedish showman, Robert Wells is another international crowd-puller, his Rhapsody in Rock show having sold over 1.7 million tickets in Scandinavia alone since 1998. The composer, pianist and live performer appeals to music lovers of all ages.

SWEDISH COMEDY

If you speak Swedish (and even if you don't) you'll get an inkling of the Swedes' self-deprecating humour by watching comedy trio, Robert Gustafsson, Henrik Schyffert and Johan Rheborg in *Killinggänget* productions past and present or the universally loved Lasse Åberg film *Sällskapsresan* (*The Charter trip*, 1980) and its follow-ups, centering on the unassuming hero, Stig-Helmer. For something a little more up-to-date, film director Josef Fares is the go-to man, bringing mixed-culture humour to Swedish comedies such as *Jalla! Jalla!* (2000), *Kopps* (2003) and *Farsan* (2010).

Below: Noomi Rapace Above: Joe Labero

> **Blockbuster Swedes on the international scene right now … Stellan Skarsgård (*Good Will Hunting*, *Pirates of the Caribbean*, Thor), Alexander Skarsgård (*True Blood*, *Melancholia*), Noomi Rapace (Girl with the Dragon Tattoo trilogy, *Prometheus*)**

SWEDISH LIVE MUSIC

Besides the big international pop artists (see chapter P), Sweden has enduring, live-act favourites, for example:

BJÖRN SKIFS
Representing Sweden in the 1978 and 1981 Eurovision song contest and continuing to have success all the way into the 2000s, including major hit, *Håll Mitt Hjärta* (Hold my heart) in 2002.

ULF LUNDELL
Sweden's answer to Bob Dylan and one of the most important figures in Swedish rock. Lundell's 1982 hit *Öppna landskap* (Open landscapes) is one of his most famous songs.

DI LEVA
Glittering robes and a Christ-like aura give Di Leva the perfect New Age appeal and his musical talent has resulted in thirty years of 'love-tastic' hits. Ask any Swede and they'll sing you: *Vi har bara varandra* (We only have each other) from 1989.

Above: Multi-talented Ulf Lundell. Not only a rock star but also an acclaimed author

Left: Di Leva, embracing the world with the music of love

...And the unusual game of kubb

Nick-named 'Viking chess' due to the element of strategy that may be employed, *kubb* is a lawn game originating from Gotland. The object is simply to knock over wooden blocks by throwing sticks at them – something that can provide hours of free fun in the summer sun.

VIKING [viːking]
VIKING

Popularly perceived as the 'bad boys' of the Dark Ages, Vikings did much more than raid and pillage the coasts of Europe and further afield. Archaeology is increasingly discovering their virtue as colonists in the lands they came to inhabit, as details of their skills in trading and craftsmanship come to light.

It was their skill at seafaring, however, that has historically been most impressive, as was their ability to endure tough conditions on board for extended periods of time. Although lacking in any type of shelter, the design of the longship was key to the success of the famous Viking voyages.

History buffs won't want to miss out on a visit to the Birka and Hovgården archeological sites near Stockholm. Together they make up one of the most complete and well-preserved examples of a Viking trading settlement through the 8th-10th Centuries, providing a wealth of information about the impact of the Vikings in Europe and the subsequent history of Scandinavia.

SECRETS OF THE LONGSHIP

In 1965, the discovery of a Viking settlement in Newfoundland gave archeologists conclusive proof that Norsemen had arrived in North America 500 years before Columbus. How did they do it?

• The superiority of Norse seafarers was due to their invention of the keel, which meant longships could be both sailed and rowed.

• A double-ended construction with symmetrical bow and stern allowed the longship to reverse direction quickly without having to turn around: particularly useful in northern latitudes where icebergs and sea ice were hazardous to navigation.

• The ship's shallow draft hull permitted navigation in waters only one metre deep, as well as beach landings – giving significant advantage when launching raids or seeking coastal shelter when conditions at sea were difficult.

V

The Karlevi runestone, on the island of Öland. These runes are unique as the only preserved example of a complete stanza of skaldic verse

MYTHS BUSTED, FUN FACTS REVEALED

- Not all Norsemen were Vikings. From the old sagas we learn that 'fara i víking' means 'to go on an expedition' and 'víkingr' referred to a seaman or warrior taking part in such a mission.

- Viking warriors did not want to die in bed because they were afraid they would go to a murky underworld called Niflheim – better to die in battle and go to Valhalla.

- We might imagine the Vikings to have been foul-smelling, murderous-looking individuals, but they were actually quite keen on personal hygiene, as is evident from the many grooming tools found in Viking burial mounds. They also bathed once a week on a Saturday. The Swedish word *lördag* (Saturday) originating from the Old Norse, originally meant 'washing day'.

- The ancient sagas refer to a precious material the Vikings used as a kind of compass called *solsten* ('sunstone'). The actual mineral they used is likely to be either calcite or iolite, both occurring abundantly in Scandinavia, and both having the required polarizing optical properties useful for navigation by the sun.

- Oval brooches are found wherever the Vikings settled. Cast in bronze and mass-produced in workshops throughout Scandinavia during the 9th and 10th Centuries, they were a favourite item of jewellery. Designs could be quite elaborate and sometimes finished with amber or glass.

WALLENBERG [val:enbærj]
WALLENBERG

You would be forgiven for thinking that IKEA's Ingvar Kamprad rules the Swedish business world but the leaders of the pack are in fact the Wallenbergs – so much so, they have a classic veal dish, *Wallenbergare* named after them. For all their financial might, however, the family does have a very important philanthropic heritage.

Descended from a prominent family of bankers, industrialists and politicians, the most famous of the Wallenbergs was Raoul Wallenberg, a diplomat who worked in Budapest during WWII to save thousands of Jews from the holocaust. Sadly, he was imprisoned by Soviet forces in 1945 and his fate remains an unsolved mystery. Raoul's humanitarian legacy lives on, however, through the foundation and institute that bear his name and the Wallenberg medal, awarded in the US since 1990 for exceptional humanitarian efforts.

*Raoul Wallenberg
as a young man*

The Wallenberg Sphere
– an empire of investment

Keeping to their motto, "Esse non Videri" (To be, not to be seen) the family maintain a low-key public profile but their influence is very much felt through the interests held by their investment companies, Investor AB and Foundation Asset Management AB. The Wallenberg Sphere encompasses names such as...

ABB GROUP

The Swiss-Swedish multinational, one of the largest engineering companies in the world.

ASTRA ZENECA PLC

The British-Swedish pharmaceuticals giant, manufacturing important drugs such as Losec and Lidocaine, to name a few.

SAS GROUP

The parent company of Scandinavian Airlines, Blue1 and Widerøe, along with other aviation services companies.

SKANDINAVISKA ENSKILDA BANKEN AB (SEB)

Founded and controlled by the Wallenberg family through Investor AB, the financial group's activities mainly revolve around banking and life insurance operations.

SAAB GROUP

From civilian security and military defence solutions to cutting-edge aeronautics, SAAB is a fundamental element of the Swedish industrial bedrock.

The production of life-saving pharmaceuticals is one area covered by the Wallenberg Sphere

SWEDISH ENTERPRISE ON THE RISE

Some of the latest Swedish start-ups seem to have shot through the stratosphere almost from 'blast off'. Here are a few:

SPOTIFY

Legally streaming and sharing copyrighted music online, the Spotify alternative to pirated music file-sharing sites has taken the world by storm. When Daniel Ek and Martin Lorentzon launched the company in 2008, they could not have envisaged having over 20 million users around the globe by 2012. Way to go!

SOLVATTEN

Saving lives has been Solvatten's business since 2006, its patented, portable water treatment unit allowing households to heat up and treat contaminated water using solar energy. Petra Wadström came up with the idea while living in Australia in 1997, now she is CEO to a company that is helping to make clean water accessible to all.

SKYPE

Founded in 2003 by Swede Niklas Zennström and Dane Janus Friis, Skype took the 'ouch' out of overseas call costs for millions of people. With free voice and video calls over the internet, Skype was so revolutionary in its inception that eBay acquired it in 2005, only for Microsoft to snap it up in 2011 for a cool USD 8,500 million.

With Solvatten saving lives, there are smiles all round

X 2000 [ækstvotusen]
X 2000

It may be over 20 years down the line now but the X 2000 high speed train certainly gave Sweden the X factor in innovation at the onset of the high-tech boom of the1990s.

Realising that it couldn't build its railway tracks as straight as the high-speed lines of Japan and France, the Swedish rail authority and rail operator (Banverket and SJ respectively) set about developing a high-speed network designed around tilting train technology. The innovation of 'soft' bogies which adjusted automatically on curves meant the train could run up to 40% faster without exerting extra stresses on the track.

X 2000 Highlights

Before the advent of the X 2000, the rail journey time between Stockholm and Gothenburg was 3h 45 mins. It now averages 3 hours.

Each train has three independent braking systems, including a magnetic track brake which can bring the train to a standstill from 200km/h in 1,100m.

X 2000 and its successors have been models for tilting train technology around the world, including Switzerland, England and China. The latest SJ 3000 train is 98% recyclable.

FROM ZIPPY ZIPPERS
TO HEADLESS HELMETS

Whether it has to do with surviving in a cold, dark, sparsely populated country or some other inherent national trait, the Swedes'
flare for innovation has been proven through history:

• Gideon Sundbäck, a Swedish American came up with the "Sep-
arable Fastener" in 1917. Where various precursors had failed,
Sundbäck made a commercial success of what we would now
recognize as a modern zip.

• In 1958, medical doctor Rune Elmqvist developed a small bat-
tery-powered pacemaker that could be inserted under the skin
of a heart patient. The world's first pacemaker operation was
carried out in Stockholm that same year; now, over 100,000
pacemakers are implanted each year in the United States alone.

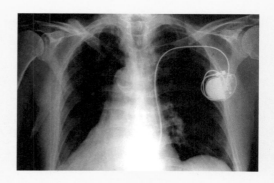

• Who says Swedes put safety before style? Industrial design stu-
dents Anna Haupt and Terese Alstin came up with the idea of a
headless bicycle helmet using airbag technology in 2005. After
winning the Swedish Venture Cup in 2006, Hövding was born,
and now fashion conscious cyclists around the world can feel
the wind in their hair, not dirt in their face…

Hövding: hi-tech safety solution for fashionistas on two wheels

YLLE [yl:æ]
WOOL

Woolly jumper, anyone? Yes, please, particularly if it's from Gotland – the rugged, romantic island off the south-eastern coast of Sweden. The indigenous sheep are the direct descendants of an ancient breed reared by the Vikings and prized for their luxurious fleece and pelt.

Lustrous, silvery and at least fifty shades of grey, Gotland fleece has always been desirable for spinning and weaving, but recently shot to 'Lord of the Rings' fame since wool from the sheep breed was used to make the magic elven cloaks for the movie trilogy. Lovely woollens are nevertheless an integral offering of the textiles industry throughout Sweden, so look out for things like:

Gotland sheep enjoy an amble along the coast

RAGGSOCKAR
Loose-fitting socks made from thick yarn, designed to be worn over ordinary socks and inside walking boots. In winter, Swedes like wearing them indoors as a substitute for slippers – very cosy!

LOVIKKAVANTAR
If you're after a signature Swedish look, a pair of *Lovikkavantar* is your best bet, their traditional design being instantly recognisable. The tradition of making these mittens originated in the village of Lovikka, in northern Sweden, after a local woman discovered a method of softening a pair of very thick woollen gloves she had knitted for a customer.

MÖSSOR
Every Swede knows you're a fool to go outside without a *mössa* (woolly hat) in winter. Choose from a startling selection of bright colours and designs – perhaps a *toppluva* (hat with a tassel) is your style?

FUNKTIONSKLÄDER
Functional clothing is big in Sweden, and quality wool products are included in the range of most Swedish sportswear brands. Try, for example, the silk-wool base layers from Houdini, or the streamlined knits and wool-mix fleeces from Fjällräven.

Speak the lingo: Helylle helt enkelt

When Swedes want to summa-
rise the character of someone
who's warm, friendly, sincere,
reliable, wouldn't hurt a fly…
a softee, they might say something like, "Han är helylle helt
enkelt"(he's simply pure wool).
The idiom is difficult to translate
precisely because it depends on
our personal evocations of wool
and its associated meaning.

ZORN [soːrn]
ZORN

Ask any Swede about their art heroes and Anders Zorn is likely to be top of the list. With a few deft strokes of his paint brush, Zorn captured the character of late 19th Century Swedish provincial life, endearing himself to the nation in his lifetime and for generations to come. It was his astonishing skill as a portrait artist that won Zorn international acclaim, however, leading to his painting famous contemporaries such as American presidents Grover Cleveland (1899) and William Taft (1911).

While Zorn's masterful depiction of the play of light on water and the female form can be enjoyed in public galleries, many of his most outstanding works are, of course, privately owned. *Sommarnöje* (1886), for example, became Sweden's priciest painting ever when it sold for SEK26 million in 2010.

Three Zorn must-sees

Ute (Outside) (1888)
Gothenburg Art Museum
Midsommardans (Midsummer Dance) (1896)
National museum*, Stockholm
Margit (1891) Zorn Collection, The Zorn museum*, Mora

*Many of Zorn's works can be seen here.

Anders Zorn, Self-portrait in Red, 1915

Margit, 1891

DALARNA – HOME TO MORE THAN ONE MASTER ARTIST

Mora enjoys it cultural heritage as birthplace, home and inspiration for Anders Zorn but the whole county of Dalarna is something of an arts and crafts hub, having generated talent through the centuries and nurtured folk traditions now recognized worldwide as symbols of Sweden as a whole.

SUNDBORN

Internationally celebrated Carl Larsson (1853-1919) and his wife Karin (1859-1928) made Lilla Hyttnäs in Sundborn one of the world's most renowned artist's homes. Art aficionados from near and far flock here to be inspired by Larsson's famous water colours and the very modern and personal design of the couple's family home.

AVESTA

The most famous Swedish accordionist of his time, Carl Jularbo (1893-1966) recorded an amazing 1,577 pieces without ever needing to learn notes. The local virtuoso's unsurpassed talent is forever commemorated at the Carl Jularbo museum, and his influence lives on in Swedish folk music tradition.

FALUN

A magnet for all things cultural long before it received its World Heritage status, the town is well-known for its arts background. Dalarnas Museum holds some of the most representative pieces of the region's folk art history, including the largest public collection of Dala horses.

The Larsson family dining room at Sundborn

ÅTERVINNING [otervin:ing]
RECYCLING

In a world where anxiety about finite resources and pollution is increasing, there is something very reassuring about a country where sustainability is an established way of life. Ever since glass bottle recycling programmes were introduced in the 1970s, Sweden has kept ahead of the game in trying to minimize the harmful impact of modern living and promote the use of renewables. Within the last decade, efforts have really paid off, with recycling rates of up to 90% for some materials now being achieved. Almost all household waste is recycled or cleanly burned, meaning very little ends up in landfill sites.

'PANTA' FOR SUSTAINABLE SUCCESS

When over 1 billion aluminium cans and 600 million PET bottles are sold in Sweden each year, optimal recycling of these drinks containers depends on an efficient, well-established deposit system – *pantsystemet*. The simple incentive of receiving money back for containers when you return them to the supermarket makes for a satisfying recycling experience and encourages school children to collect 'litter' as a cool way of raising cash. Novel advertising has also helped, the 'Pantamera' (return more!) campaign, for example, being a fun way of encouraging the public to be environmentally conscious.

Watch out for...

...the KRAV and SVANEN labels in Sweden if you want to make eco-friendly purchases. The KRAV label certifies organic products free from chemical pesticides, fertilizers or genetically modified organisms while SVANEN (Swan label) is an official eco-label for the whole Nordic region, guaranteeing that the environmental impact of goods and services throughout their lifecycle has been examined and approved.

SWITCHED ON SWEDEN
CUTS CARBON FOOTPRINT

A cold climate and a high standard of living means Swedes are big energy users, but how do they manage to keep carbon emissions down?

NUCLEAR AND HYDROELECTRIC POWER
Approximately 85% of electricity in Sweden comes from these two sources, neither of which generates carbon emissions.

DISTRICT HEATING
Since the introduction of *fjärrvärme* (district heating) in 1990, carbon emissions have been declining. Heat produced by the clean burning of household waste and biofuels, for example, is piped directly to homes and other buildings within a specific geographical area. Half of all Sweden's heating needs are now met through district heating and the burning of waste accounts for over 20% of district heating in the country.

ENERGY-EFFICIENT CONSTRUCTION
Triple glazing has been standard issue in Swedish house construction for many years now, but there is no end to improving energy efficiency. The concept of 'passive houses', the product of Swedish and German research in the late 1980s, is increasingly becoming a residential reality in Sweden and elsewhere in Europe. Compared to a conventional build with an average heating demand of 150kWh/m2a, these homes need only 15kWh/m2a – that's 90% less!

> **The average Swede releases 5.3 tons of carbon dioxide per year into the atmosphere, compared with the EU average of 8.1 tons and the US average of 19.0 tons***
>
> **All figures US department of energy, 2009*

*The Akkats hydropower station on the Lule Älv river,
outside Jokkmokk, famous for its monumental paint-
ings by Bengt Lindström and Lars Pirak*

ÄRTSOPPA [ætsop:a]
PEA SOUP

Traditionally served on Thursdays in Swedish schools and in the military, *ärtsoppa* is a classic, simple dish that has been eaten in Sweden for centuries. This thick, nourishing soup made with yellow peas and ham was one of August Strindberg's absolute favourites, and many Swedes would agree, although it may also have to do with the fact that pancakes with berry jam and whipped cream are usually served afterwards!

Hearty, traditional dishes such as pea soup are known as *husmanskost*. In Sweden of old, a *husman* was a commoner, and so the cheap and basic food he ate came to be known as husmanskost. Over the years, transforming plain old simple grub into modern must-have gourmet fare has required a bit of inspired help, however. Indeed, Sweden was something of a gastronomic desert until the 1950s and 60s, when restaurateur extraordinaire, Tore Wretman kick-started a national cooking revival through his radio and TV shows. Suddenly, everyone wanted to make traditional food with fresh local ingredients and a modern twist.

PYTTIPANNA, LAXPUDDING AND OTHER HUSMANS

Go to any Swedish pub or restaurant and you will almost certainly find these classic dishes or variations thereof:

PYTTIPANNA

Pan-fried cubes of meat and potato with chopped onion (traditionally left-overs) served with a fried egg and pickled beetroot. A creamy version of this dish is called *gräddstuvad pyttipanna*.

LAXPUDDING/LAXLÅDA

Another dish usually made at home from leftovers – this time with boiled potatoes and salmon. The main ingredients are layered with onion, dill, egg and cream and baked.

SKAGENRÖRA

Tore Wretman's creation is a staple on any Swedish café lunch menu. This dill-flavoured prawn mayonnaise is popular as Toast Skagen or to go with a baked potato.

PANNBIFF

The posh cousin of the famous Swedish *köttbullar* (meatballs), *pannbiff* is basically a pan-fried beef patty served with potatoes, an onion sauce and the quintessential condiments, *inlagd gurka* (pickled cucumbers) and *lingonsylt* (lingonberry jam).

RÅRAKA/RAGGMUNK

Deliciously crisp and light when expertly prepared, *råraka* is a large fried potato cake often served in restaurants with bleak roe, crème fraîche and red onion. At home, Swedes might serve it with pan-fried pork and lingonberry jam, as they would *raggmunk*, which is similar but heavier because it is made with pancake batter.

ÄRTSOPPA RECIPE

A one-pot wonder for a hungry family. This pea soup recipe serves 4.

INGREDIENTS
500g yellow peas – pre-soaked the day before
1.5 litres of water
300g piece of salted pork or a ham hock
1 peeled onion, studded with 2 whole cloves
1 carrot
1 tsp dried thyme
1tsp dried marjoram
2 tbsp Skåne mustard (or any brown, coarse-grain mustard)
5 whole peppercorns

1. Bring the peas to the boil in a large pot of water before adding the remaining ingredients, apart from the mustard.

2. Cook the peas until they are soft (about 1½ hours) but take out the pork before this, if it is tender. Stir the peas occasionally and remove any froth and pea shells from the surface of the soup.

3. You may have to add more water, depending on how thick you want the soup.

4. Cut the pork into pieces once the soup looks like it's almost ready, dividing it among your serving bowls.

5. Season the soup with 2 tablespoons of mustard just as it has finished cooking.

6. Serve with a little mustard on the side and enjoy with your favourite type of bread.